Scary Creatures

BATS

Written by
Daniel Gilpin

Illustrated by
Bob Hersey

W
FRANKLIN WATTS
A Division of Scholastic Inc.

NEW YORK • TORONTO • LONDON • AUCKLAND • SYDNEY
MEXICO CITY • NEW DELHI • HONG KONG
DANBURY, CONNECTICUT

Created and designed by
David Salariya

Author:

Daniel Gilpin studied zoology at Bristol University in England, before becoming a professional natural history author. This is his tenth book.

Artist:

Bob Hersey has worked in many mediums, including designing 3-dimensional models, artwork for advertising, and illustrating children's books. He lives in Sevenoaks, Kent, England.

Additional Artists:
Carolyn Scrace
David Stewart

Series Creator:

David Salariya was born in Dundee, Scotland. In 1989, he established The Salariya Book Company. He has illustrated a wide range of books and has created many new series for publishers in the U.K. and overseas. He lives in Brighton, England, with his wife, illustrator Shirley Willis, and their son.

Editor: Karen Barker Smith

Assistant Editor: Michael Ford

Picture Research: Matt Packer

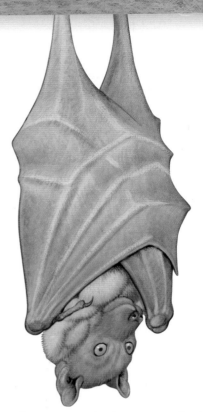

Created, designed, and produced by
The Salariya Book Company Ltd
Book House
25 Marlborough Place
Brighton BN1 1UB

Visit the Salariya Book Company at
www.salariya.com

A CIP catalog record for this title is available from the Library of Congress.

ISBN 0-531-12375-8 (Lib. Bdg.)
ISBN 0-531-16746-1 (Pbk.)

Published in 2004 in the United States by
Franklin Watts
An imprint of Scholastic Library Publishing
90 Sherman Turnpike
Danbury, CT 06816

Printed in China.

Printed on paper from sustainable forests.

Photo Credits:

Bettman/CORBIS: 27
Getty Images: 24
Melvin Grey /NHPA: 13, 21
Daniel Heuclin/NHPA: 7, 8, 21, 23
Christoph Kappel/naturepl.com: 5
Hugh Maynard/naturepl.com: 26bottom
Mountain High Maps/©1993 Digital Wisdom Inc: 28-29
Dietmar Nill/naturepl.com: 15
Richard T. Nowitz/CORBIS: 26top
Tim Page/CORBIS: 7
©Merlin D Tuttle, bat conservation international: 18
Rod Planck/NHPA: 25
Adrian Warren/Last Refuge Ltd: 16

Every effort has been made to trace copyright holders. The Salariya Book Company apologizes for any unintentional omissions and would be pleased, in such cases, to add an acknowledgment in future editions.

2/04

Contents

What Is a Bat? 4

How Big Are Bats? 6

How Do Bats Fly? 8

What's Inside a Bat? 11

Can Bats Walk? 12

What Do Bats Eat? 14

How Do Bats Hunt? 16

Why Do Bats Hang Upside Down? 18

Do Bats Hibernate? 21

Are Vampire Bats Real? 22

Can Bats Spread Disease? 24

Why Are Bats Scary? 26

Bats Around the World 28

Bat Facts 30

Glossary 31

Index 32

What Is a Bat?

A bat is a flying **mammal**. Mammals feed their young on milk. Most of them also have hair or fur. Bats are the only mammals that can fly, although some mammals can glide.

Is a bat a mammal?

Yes, a bat is a mammal.

Is a mouse a mammal?

Yes, a mouse is a mammal.

Like bats, mice feed their young on milk and have a coat of fur. Mice belong to a group of mammals called **rodents**, which also includes squirrels and rats. Rodents' front teeth grow throughout their lives. They keep their teeth worn down by gnawing.

Is a butterfly a mammal?

Butterflies have wings and can fly like bats can, but they are not mammals. Butterfly young, or caterpillars, feed themselves. They eat leaves. A butterfly is an insect. Like all insects, it has six legs.

No, a butterfly is an insect.

Pallidus bat in flight

Did You Know?

There are more than 950 different **species** of bat in the world. Thirteen species of bat are **endangered**.

There are two main types of bat. The smaller type eats insects or meat. The larger type feeds on fruit or **nectar** from flowers. The bat pictured above hunts flying insects, such as moths.

How Big Are Bats?

The world's smallest bat is Kitti's hog-nosed bat (above). It measures just 1 inch (3 cm) long and weighs just 2 grams. This type of bat is so tiny that it could sit on your finger.

Bats come in lots of different sizes. Most of them are small, not much bigger than a mouse with wings. North America's biggest bat, the western mastiff bat, has a wingspan of 22 inches (56 cm). The smallest in North America, the common pipistrelle, measures around 1.5 inches (4 cm).

Did You Know?

Kitti's hog-nosed bat was not discovered until 1973. Not only is it the world's smallest bat, but it is also the world's smallest mammal.

The biggest bats eat fruit. They are known as fruit bats. Fruit bats live in hot countries where their food grows year-round. They eat at night and spend the day hanging from tree branches.

Spotted bat

The spotted bat from western North America is a medium-sized insect-eating species. It has a wingspan of 14 inches (35 cm). Its huge, pink ears are the largest of any North American bat. At 2 inches (5 cm) in length, its ears are almost as long as its body!

The largest fruit bats are known as flying foxes. Although they are not as big as a real fox, they are very large. The world's biggest bat is the kalong, a type of flying fox from Indonesia. Its wings measure more than 5 feet (1.5 m) from one tip to another. The Indian flying fox is another large bat (left).

Indian flying fox

Bats' wings are much longer than their bodies. This boy is holding a fruit bat (below), showing its large wingspan.

Boy with a fruit bat, showing its wingspan

How Do Bats Fly?

Bats fly the same way birds and insects do — they flap their wings. As a bat's wings flap downward, they push against the air underneath them. This forces the bat up. On the upstroke, the bat turns its wings at an angle so they slice through the air.

A bird's bones support muscles, from which feathers grow.

A bat's bones support skin, like the crossed poles on a kite.

Comparison between a bird's wing and a bat's wing

X-Ray Vision

Hold the next page up to the light and see what's inside a Natterer's bat.

See what's inside

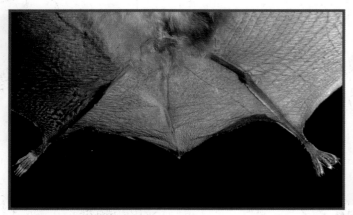

Skin stretched between the legs and tail of a bat

Bats' wings are made from thin membranes of skin stretched between the body, legs, and long finger bones. In some bats, the wing membrane also stretches between the legs and tail (left). Most bats have four fingers built into the wing membrane. The fifth finger, or thumb, forms a claw which the bat uses to help it crawl around.

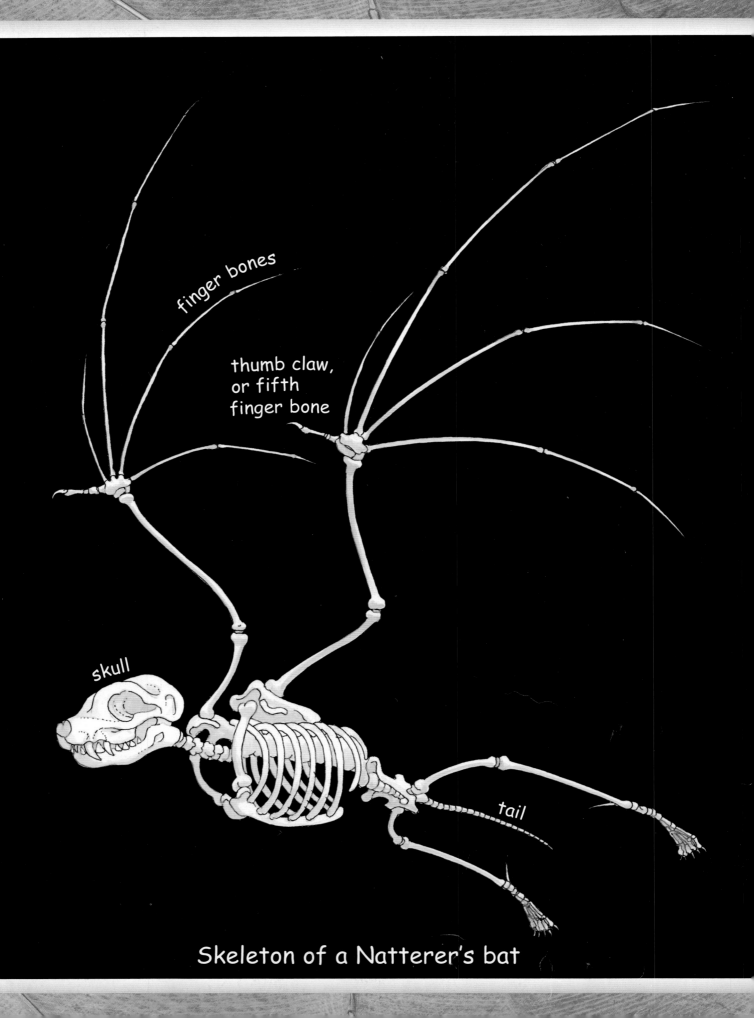

finger bones

thumb claw,
or fifth
finger bone

skull

tail

Skeleton of a Natterer's bat

Fringe-lipped bat from South America, about to eat a tree frog

lung   ribs   intestines

wing membrane

What's Inside a Bat?

Bats have the same kinds of bones as humans, although bat bones are much smaller than ours. The leg bones of bats stick out behind their narrow hips and help support their wings, arm bones, and long, slender fingers.

Did You Know?

There is no such thing as being "blind as a bat." All bats can see, and some, such as flying foxes, have very good eyesight.

What are bats' teeth like?

Insect-eaters have small, pointed teeth for crunching up their **prey**. Bats that hunt larger animals have long **canines** for stabbing. Most fruit bats have large, flat **molars** for crushing. Vampire bats have very sharp teeth for slicing through skin.

Different kinds of bats have different teeth.

Can Bats Walk?

Many bats cannot walk and avoid landing on the ground, but some insect-eating bats can scurry along if they have to. If they do end up on the ground, it is very difficult for them to take off again. There is one group of bats that lands on the ground all the time — vampire bats. They feed on the blood of large animals and usually creep up to their prey quietly.

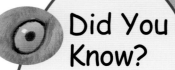

Did You Know?

In 1993, a new species of bat was discovered in Britain. Called the soprano pipistrelle, it looks very similar to the common pipistrelle but makes higher pitched squeaks and has lighter colored fur.

Unlike most bats, vampire bats can use their wings like another pair of legs. After landing silently near their sleeping prey, they slowly walk on all fours toward it (see 1 and 2 below).

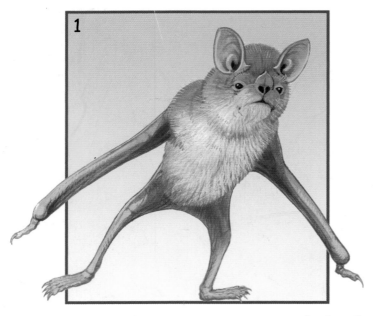

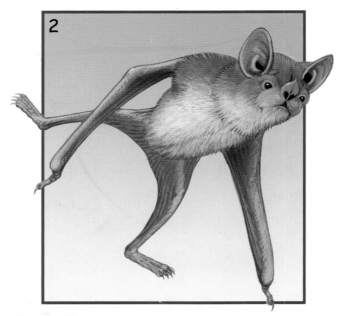

A bat's movements while "walking"

Common pipistrelle bat crawling over a rock

If they need to, vampire bats can also hop and leap over the ground (see 3 and 4 below).

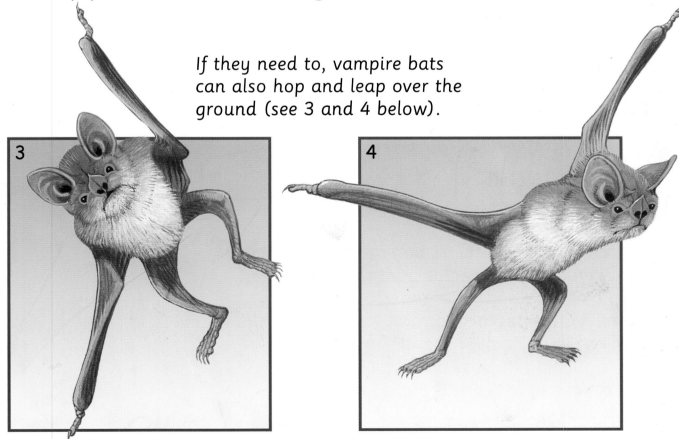

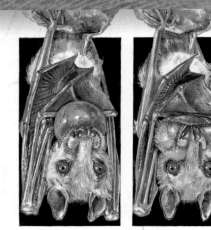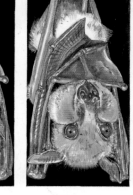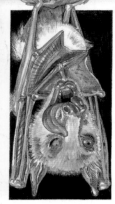

Wahlberg's epauletted bat eating a fig

Most fruit bats **roost** in trees by day and look for their food at night. Wahlberg's epauletted bat (left), from Africa, feeds on figs. The bat takes the figs to a safe perch and eats them while hanging upside down.

What Do Bats Eat?

Bats eat a wide variety of food. Most of the smaller species feed on insects, such as moths, but some hunt animals almost as large as themselves. Vampire bats live entirely on a diet of blood. There are even bats that feed on fish. Flying foxes and their relatives eat fruit that can be found in forests. Other bats feed on nectar from flowers, licking it out with their long tongues.

North America's southern long-nosed bat (right) feeds on nectar from the flowers of cacti and other desert plants. Sometimes it lands on the plant, but usually it hovers over it, dipping its nose and long tongue in to reach the sweet, sticky food.

Southern long-nosed bat

Fringe-lipped bat, eating a frog

Fringe-lipped bats (above) only hunt frogs that are harmless. All frogs have their own call and this bat ignores those of poisonous species. The fringe-lipped bat is one of several bats that hunts large prey.

The Australian ghost bat kills and eats frogs, lizards, mice, birds, and even other bats. It hunts in the trees and undergrowth, often flying low over the ground. Small creatures may be eaten without landing, but larger prey is usually taken back to the roost in a cave or hollow tree.

How Do Bats Hunt?

Bats hunt at night, in the dark. Although bats can see, most rely on other senses to find their prey. Insect-eating bats catch moths in midair by using echolocation. They emit high-pitched squeaks and clicks, and then wait to hear if any echoes return to them. If the sound wave from a squeak or click bumps into a moth, some of the sound will bounce back. Most insect-eating bats' ears are tuned to pick up these echoes from prey.

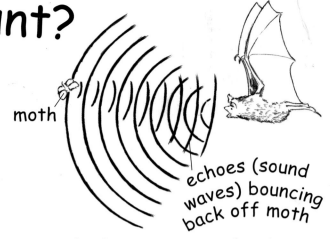

moth

echoes (sound waves) bouncing back off moth

Using echolocation to find prey

By measuring the time from click to echo, a bat's brain is able to figure out how far away a moth is (above). If the echoes from repeated clicks start returning faster, the bat knows that it is getting closer to its prey. If the echoes take longer to return, it knows the moth is moving away.

Most insect-eating bats have very sensitive hearing. Their huge ears act as funnels, **amplifying** sound.

Many echolocating bats make sounds through their nostrils. Some, such as this giant spear-nosed bat (right), have specially shaped noses thought to help change or focus the sounds.

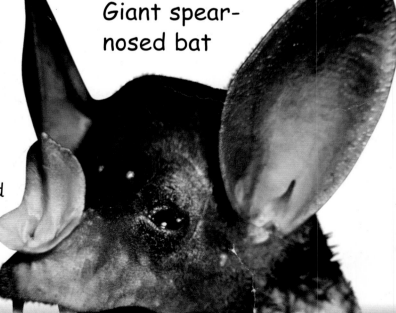

Giant spear-nosed bat

16

False vampire bat catching a mouse

It is not just insect-eaters that use echolocation. Bats that hunt larger animals use it, too. This false vampire bat (above) uses echolocation to home in on a mouse, which it then takes back to its roost to eat.

Did You Know?

Bats can "see" using echolocation. As well as helping them hunt, they use it to avoid obstacles, such as other bats, when flying in the dark.

Why Do Bats Hang Upside Down?

Bats hang upside down because of the way their legs are positioned. A bat's legs stick out from the back of its body. This helps hold the bat's wings open in flight. Many bats find it almost impossible to stand up and take off from a flat surface because of this. To get into the air, they take off by dropping from a branch or ledge.

The claws on bats' toes are shaped like hooks (see next page). Most fruit bats use their hooked toes to hang from the branches of trees. Because they are lighter, smaller bats can grip tiny overhangs and ledges on the roofs of caves.

X-Ray Vision

Hold the next page up to the light and see what's inside a flying fox.

See what's inside

Spectacled flying fox

Bats have a hook-shaped claw on the thumb bone of their wings (below). They use this claw to help them move around while hanging upside down (above).

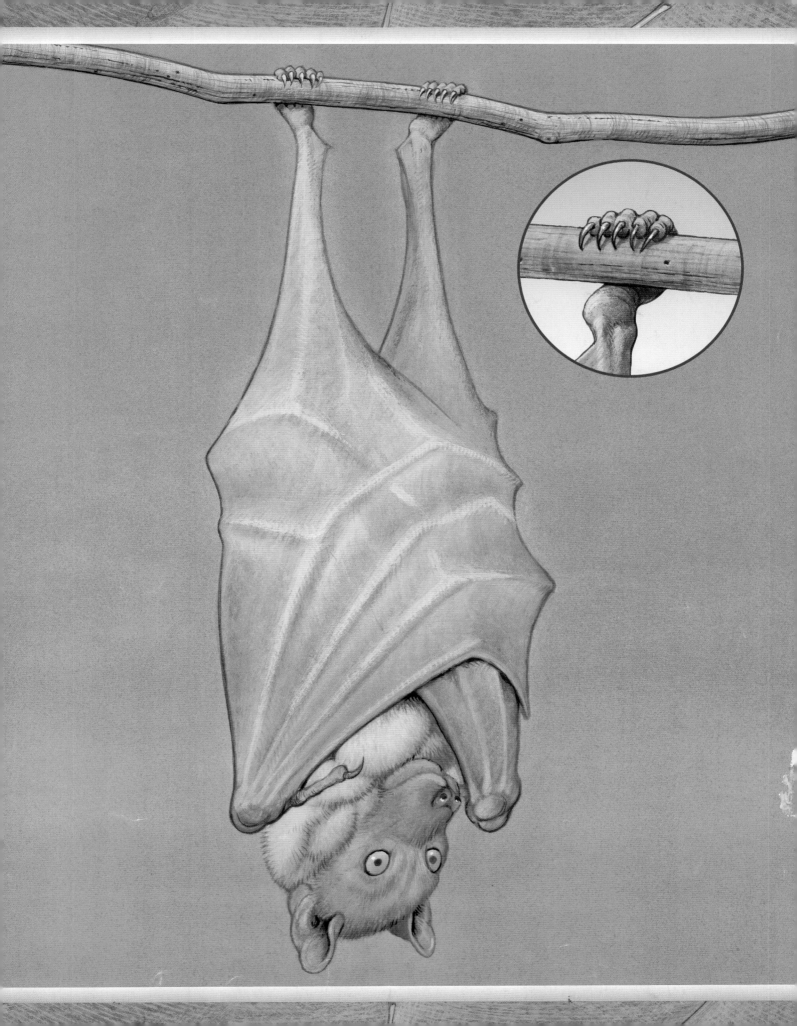

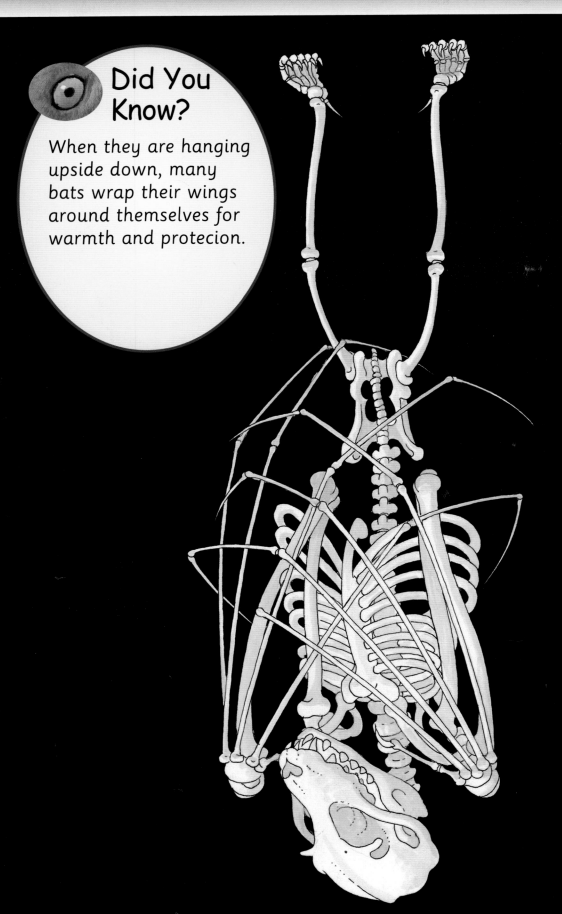

Did You Know?

When they are hanging upside down, many bats wrap their wings around themselves for warmth and protecion.

Skeleton of a flying fox with its wings wrapped around itself

Do Bats Hibernate?

Some bats **hibernate** in the winter to save energy. When hibernating, bats have a much lower heart rate than when they are active. Their body temperatures drop, sometimes as low as 32° fahrenheit (0° celsius) — the freezing point of water. When hibernating, bats can survive for months on their fat reserves. If they did not hibernate, most bats in cold climates would starve to death at this time of year since food is often hard to find.

Did You Know?

Few bats hibernate in places with extremely cold winters, such as Canada and north-eastern Europe. Instead, most fly south in autumn to warmer places and hibernate there.

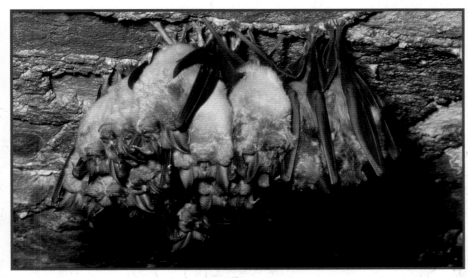

Greater horseshoe bats roosting

Greater horseshoe bats hibernate huddled together for warmth. These greater horseshoes (left) are just roosting — when they hibernate, they wrap their wings around their bodies.

The mouth of a common vampire bat

Are Vampire Bats Real?

Vampire bats are real, but they are not something to worry about. Vampire bats feed on the blood of other animals. All three species of vampire bat live in South and Central America. Two species are rare and usually hunt roosting birds. The third species, the common vampire bat, gets its meals from mammals, including humans.

How do vampire bats eat?

To eat, vampire bats cut out a small piece of flesh from their prey with their razor-sharp teeth. Then they lap up the blood as it flows from the wound. The bat's saliva prevents the blood from clotting before they finish their meal.

Did You Know?

Vampire bats must drink half their own body weight in blood every day to survive. Bats too ill to hunt are fed by other **colony** members, which **regurgitate** blood for them when they return.

Vampire bats drink blood from their prey.

Vampire bats search for their prey by sight, smell, and echolocation. Once a bat has found a victim, it uses its heat-sensitive nose to locate an area rich in blood vessels before it bites.

Vampire bat with outstretched wings

23

Can Bats Spread Disease?

Most bats are harmless but some can spread disease. The worst disease that bats carry is rabies, which is deadly to humans if left untreated. In North America, few people are ever bitten by bats, so the risk of catching rabies from one is very small.

Did You Know?

In 1991, vampire bats caused a rabies **epidemic** in a town in Brazil. Driven from their natural homes by logging, several colonies of the bats descended on the town one night.

Leaf-nosed bat

However, in other parts of the world, the chance of catching rabies from a vampire bat bite is very high. Every year, dozens of people in South America catch rabies from vampire bats. The numbers would be much higher if humans were the bats' main prey, but most vampire bats feed on wild animals or livestock such as cattle.

Most bats have teeth sharp enough to break the skin if they bite. Usually though, the only people who get bitten by bats are those who work with them, such as scientists and **conservationists**. These people have regular shots to prevent them from developing rabies.

Like vampire bats, mosquitoes feed on blood. In tropical countries, many mosquitoes carry the disease malaria and pass it from bats to humans.

Mosquito feeding on a person

A model bat used to frighten people at Halloween

Bats are creatures of the night that roost in churches and abandoned tombs. They have long been linked with Halloween.

Why Are Bats Scary?

People who are afraid of bats usually do not understand them. They think that bats might be dangerous animals that could attack them, or they just think they look frightening. Some people are scared of bats because of stories they have heard. For instance, it has been said that bats sometimes fly into women's hair and get tangled up. This story is made up, but many people still believe such stories.

Hammer-headed fruit bats (right), found in Asia, Northern Australasia, and Africa, are one of the strangest looking bats. However, they are completely harmless to humans.

Scene from the 1922 vampire film *Nosferatu*

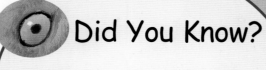 Did You Know?

Vampire bats grind their teeth together to keep them razor sharp. A vampire bat's bite is painless to its prey.

Centuries ago, bats were often linked with witchcraft and the devil. More recently they have become tied to tales of vampires. The idea of human vampires turning into bats was invented by the Irish writer Bram Stoker in his novel *Dracula*, published in 1897. The first film based on Stoker's book was called *Nosferatu* (above). Released in 1922, it featured a very bat-like vampire.

Bats Around the World

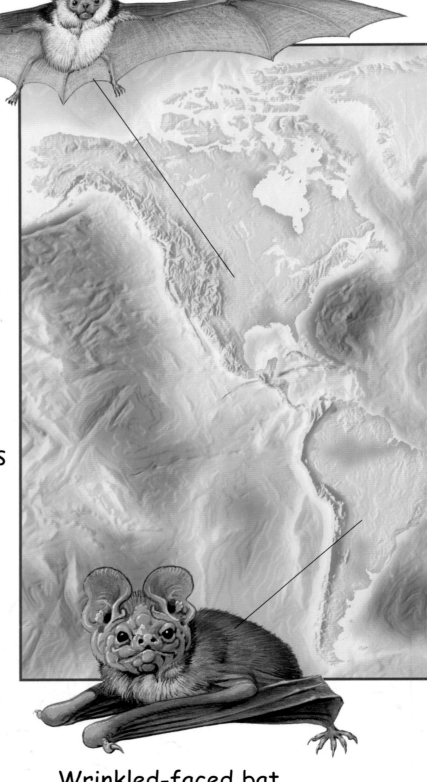

Spotted bat

Bats live all over the world and can be found on every **continent** except Antarctica. Bats make up about a quarter of all mammal species. They are usually the first mammals to appear on new islands after they are created by volcanoes. On many islands they are still the only mammals today.

Wrinkled-faced bat

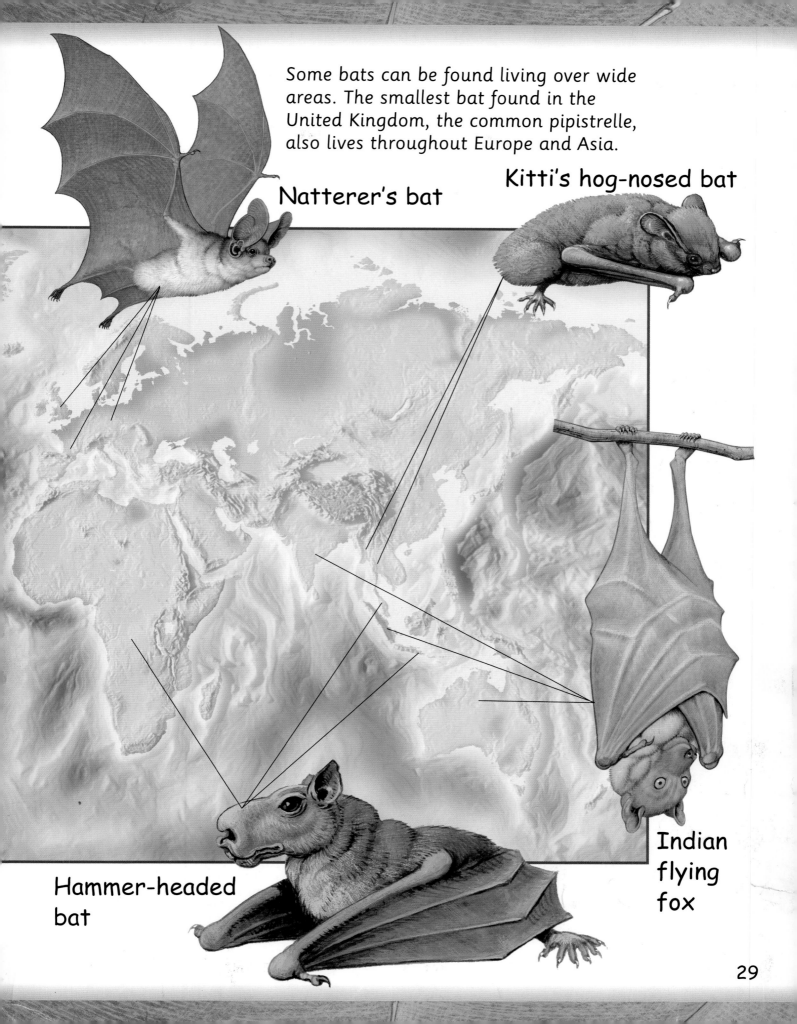

Some bats can be found living over wide areas. The smallest bat found in the United Kingdom, the common pipistrelle, also lives throughout Europe and Asia.

Natterer's bat

Kitti's hog-nosed bat

Hammer-headed bat

Indian flying fox

Bat Facts

Bats' wings heal very fast. Holes repair themselves in a matter of days. Even their finger bones heal very quickly if broken.

The fishing bat of South America catches fish from rivers at night. Using echolocation, it detects the ripples that fish produce when they are at the surface. Then it flies over the water's surface, dragging the hooked claws of its feet through the water to grab its prey.

More than three-quarters of all bats are insect-eaters.

The largest flying foxes have wingspans of up to 7 feet (2 m).

Some insect-eating bats have membranes of skin between their legs and tail, which they use to scoop flying moths from the air.

The smallest bat, Kitti's hog-nosed bat, has a wingspan of just 3 inches (8 cm).

Honduran white bats make waterproof shelters by gnawing along the mid-ribs of large leaves. The sides of the leaves flop down, forming tent-like structures. The bats roost under the leaves, which keep them safe from tropical downpours.

Most bats roost and give birth in colonies. The largest known bat colony forms each summer in a huge cave near San Antonio, Texas. As many as 20 million Mexican free-tailed bats gather there to give birth.

Some bats use their thumb claws to handle food. Male flying foxes also use them for fighting. Fruit bats can use their feet and hooked thumbs to climb "hand over hand" beneath branches.

The Rodrigues flying fox lives on the tiny island of Rodrigues in the Indian Ocean and is found nowhere else in the world.

South America's fringe-lipped bat specializes in hunting frogs. It finds its food by listening for the calls of male frogs, which croak through the night to attract females.

Some fruit bats raid banana plantations and other places where tropical fruit is grown, making the bats unpopular with farmers. However, without bats, many of these fruits would not grow in the first place — nectar-eating bats are often the main **pollinators** of tropical fruit trees.

Glossary

amplify To turn up or increase a sound.

canines The four pointed teeth mammals have in-between their incisors and molars.

colony A group of animals living together.

conservationist A person who works to protect wildlife or wild places.

continent A very large landmass. There are seven continents: North America, South America, Europe, Africa, Asia, Australia, and Antarctica.

endangered A plant or animal in danger of becoming extinct.

epidemic A widespread outbreak of a disease.

hibernate To sleep through the winter.

mammal An animal that feeds on its mother's milk when it is a baby.

molars Back teeth used for grinding or chewing.

nectar A sweet, sticky liquid produced by flowers to attract animals.

pollinator An animal or object that takes pollen from a male flower to a female flower so that seeds and fruit will form.

prey Any animal that is hunted by other animals for food.

regurgitate To bring up food from the stomach to the mouth.

rodent A small mammal with gnawing teeth such as a mouse, rat, or squirrel.

roost A place to rest or sleep.

species A group of living things that look alike, behave in the same way, and can interbreed.

Index

A
Australian ghost bat 15

B
bones 8, 11
butterflies 4

C
common pipistrelle bat
6, 12, 13, 29

D
Dracula 27

E
eagles 4
echolocation 16-17, 30

F
fishing bat 30
false vampire bat 17
feeding 5, 6, 11, 12,
14-15, 17
flight 8
flying fox 18-19, 20, 30
Indian flying fox 7, 29
Rodrigues flying fox
30
fringe-lipped bat 11,
15, 30
fruit bat 6-7, 18, 30
hammer-headed fruit
bat 26, 29

G
giant spear-nosed bat 16
greater horseshoe bat 21

H
Halloween 26
hearing 16
hibernation 21, 31
Honduran white bat 30
hunting 16

I
insects 5, 11, 14

K
kalong 7
kitti's hog-nosed bat 6,
29, 30

L
leaf-nosed bat 24

M
malaria 25
Mexican free-tailed bat
30
mosquitoes 25

N
Natterer's bat 8-9, 10,
29
nectar 5, 31
Nosferatu 27

P
pallidus bat 5
pollination 30-31

R
rabies 24
rodents 4, 31
roosting 15, 17, 21,
30-31

S
skin 8
soprano pipistrelle bat
12
southern long-nosed bat
14
spectacled flying fox
18
spotted bat 6, 28

T
teeth 11, 31
tree frog 11

V
vampire bat 11, 12-13,
14, 22-23, 24-25, 27
vision 11

W
Wahlberg's epauletted
bat 14
walking 12
wings 8
wrinkled-faced bat 28